FANTASIA ON
POLISH CHRISTMAS CAROLS

A MEDLEY OF 7 TRADITIONAL "KOLENDY"
FOR LATE INTERMEDIATE PIANO SOLO

ARRANGED BY CHRISTOS TSITSAROS

Cover image: Church of SS. Peter and Paul, Krakow, from 'Klejnoty Miasta Krakowa',
published 1899 (colour litho) by Juliusza & Tondosa Kossaka, Stanislawa (fl.1899)

Private Collection/ The Stapleton Collection/ The Bridgeman Art Library

ISBN 978-1-4584-1188-4

7777 W. BLUEMOUND RD. P.O. BOX 13819 MILWAUKEE, WI 53213

In Australia Contact:
Hal Leonard Australia Pty. Ltd.
4 Lentara Court
Cheltenham, Victoria, 3192 Australia
Email: ausadmin@halleonard.com.au

Visit Hal Leonard Online at
www.halleonard.com

Christmas holds a unique place in the hearts of Polish people, as it presents an opportunity to unite in peace, love, and forgiveness, and to express deep reverence for the Christ Child. The "Kolendy" (Christmas Carols) perfectly embody this spirit of generosity and good will, and accompany formal religious celebrations, as well as home gatherings and festivities often lasting several days. Their wonderful folk flavor and typically Polish emotional character, ranging from sad to humorous and tender, provided the inspiration for this Fantasia on Christmas Carols, in which a series of seven "Kolendy" are threaded together through key relationships and transitional elaborative sections.

–Christos Tsitsaros

LYRICS TO THE "KOLENDY"

IN THE STILL OF THE NIGHT
(Wśród Nocney Ciszy)

(mm. 1–28)

Angels from heaven, sang a thrilling psalm,

Walking the shepherds from their drowsy calm.

Rise ye shepherds, hurry onward,

Greet the new born Son of David, King Emmanuel!

They found the Savior with His Mother mild,

Laid in the manger, Infant Jesus Child.

Bow ye shepherds to the Christ King,

Bring to Him your humble offering King Emmanuel!

QUICKLY ON TO BETHLEHEM
(Przybieżeli do Betlejem)

(mm. 29–46)

Quickly on to Bethlehem the shepherds came,

Playing gaily on their lutes to bless His Name.

Glory to God on Highest, Glory to God on Highest

And on earth, peace to men.

Giving their respects to all humility,

To the Infant Jesus from hearts lovingly,

Glory to God on Highest, Glory to God on Highest

And on earth, peace to men.

HASTEN YONDER
(Pójdźmy Wszyscy)

(mm. 47–73)

To the stable, hasten yonder,

To adore this Holy Wonder,

Babe of heaven, like no other,

Virgin Mary, sweetest Mother,

Babe of heaven, like no other,

Virgin Mary, Sweetest Mother.

Oh, Babe Jesus, we adore Thee,

Twice your birth to us has brought Thee,

[Once of God, through all the ages,

Now of Mary, told by sages.:]

IN A MANGER
(W Żłobie Leży)

(mm. 73–95)

In a manger sleeps the Infant,

Hasten all to find Him there.

Little Jesus, to us heav'n sent,

Blessings with us all to share.

Hurry, shepherds, kneel before Him,

Play sweet music like Seraphim

Worship Him as Lord and King.

We shall follow, singing our song,
Bringing homage, gifts of prayer,
Little Savior, bless this large throng,
Watch us with loving care.
Hurry, children, see Him sleeping,
Holy parents watch are keeping,
So let us all adore Him.

May the whole world ring with gladness
At the tidings of His birth.
Truth and light dispel the sadness,
Joy rings out, songs fill the earth.
Hurry, praise the Child before us
Join the Cherubim's glad chorus,
Glorify our God on high.

JESUS, TINY BABY
(Jesus Malusieńki)

(mm. 96–132)

Jesus Blessed wonder,
Lay in lowly manger,
With cold trembling, while beside Him
Mother's heart was aching.

Mary was resourceful,
Covered with head shawl,
Then with fresh hay wrapped Him gently
Kept him warm on this day.
Jesus had no cradle,
Nor a downy pillow,
So in small crib Mary placed Him
On hay, soft and mellow.

LULLABY, SWEET JESUS
(Lulajże Jezuniu)

(mm. 133–165)

Lullaby, sweet Jesus, pearl very precious,
Lullaby sweet Jesus, sleep now, Your cries hush.
Lullaby, sweet Jesus, lullaby Baby,
Sleep Infant beloved, Mother will lull Thee.

Close now Your wee eyelids, blinking with soft tears,
Still Your wee lips trembling, for slumber time nears.
Lullaby, sweet Jesus, lullaby, baby,
Sleep Infant beloved, Mother will lull Thee.

CHRIST IS BORN
(Gdy Się Chrystus Rodzi)

(mm. 166-189)

Christ the king is born, on an early morn,
Radiant glows the dark night, Skies aflame with bright light,
All the angels are rejoicing, Heavenly music, they are voicing,
Gloria, gloria, gloria, in excelsis Deo!

Angels told the shepherds,
Keeping watch o'er their herds,
"Follow ye the bright star,
Bethlehem is not far,
For the Savior there is born
To the world this early morn,
Gloria, Gloria, Gloria, in excelsis Deo!"

Fantasia on Polish Christmas Carols

To Professor Jan Ekier

Arranged by Christos Tsitsaros

In the Still of the Night (W ród Nocney Ciszy)

Moderato comodo

Quickly On to Bethlehem (Przybie eli do Betlejem)

29 Allegro vivace e con spirito

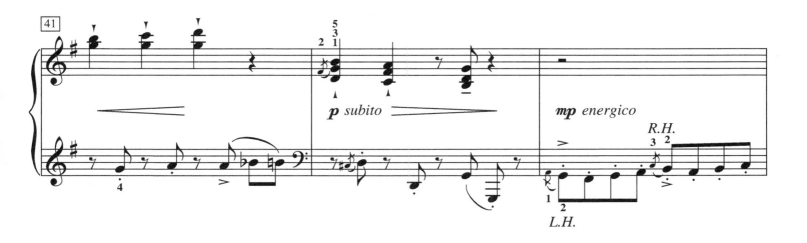

Hasten Yonder (Pójd my Wszyscy)

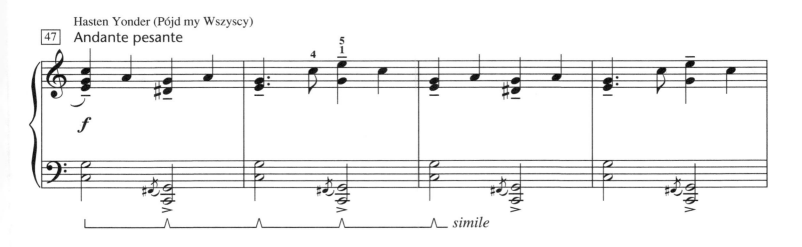

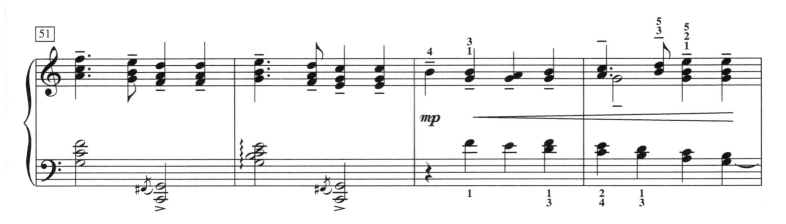

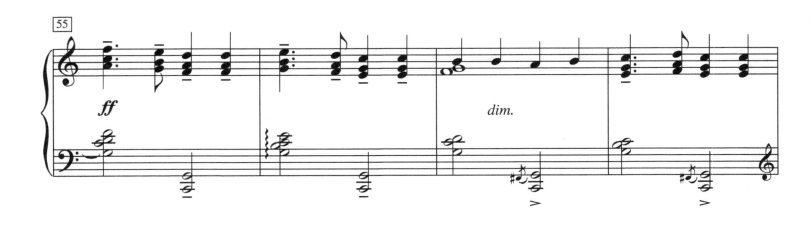

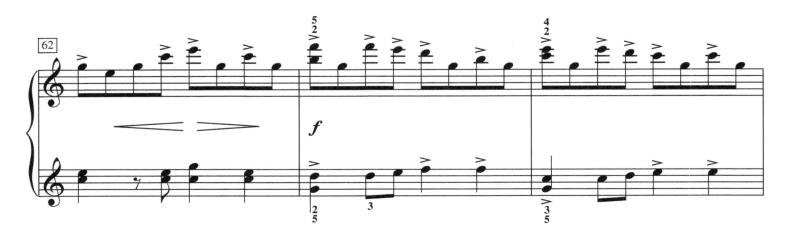

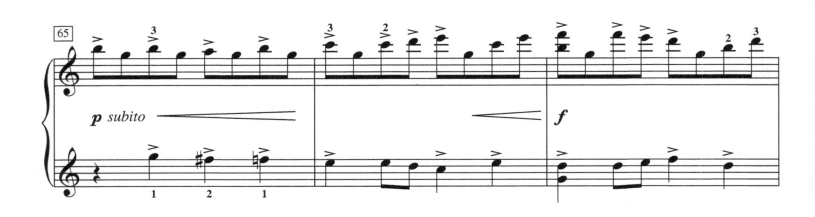

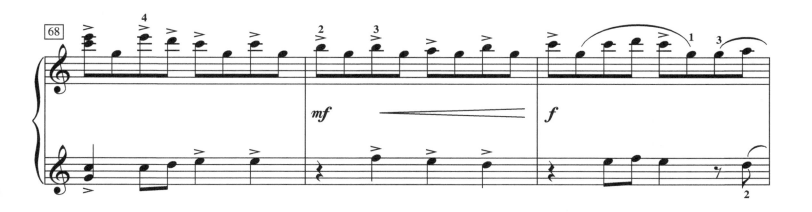

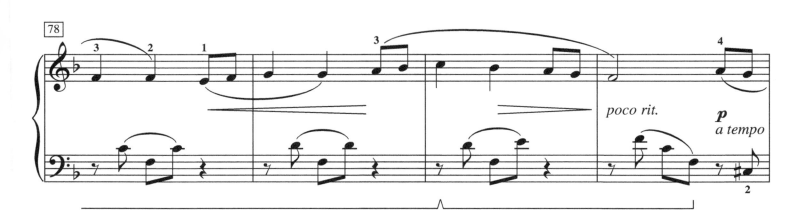

In a Manger (W łobie Leży)

Moderato pastorale

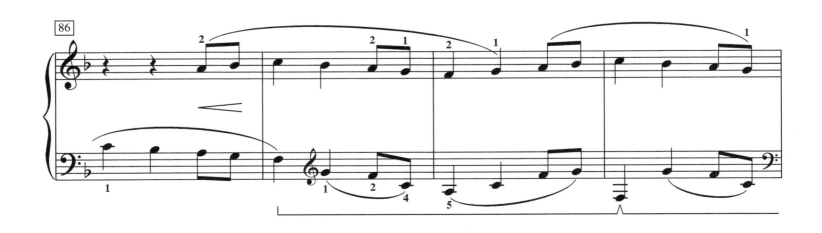

Jesus, Tiny Baby (Jesus Malusie ki)

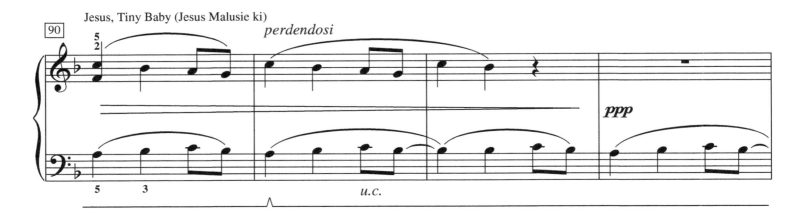

Poco lento

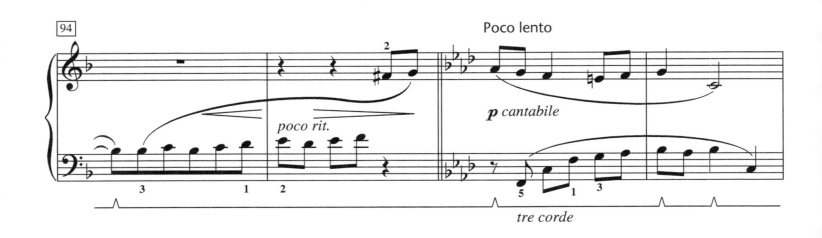

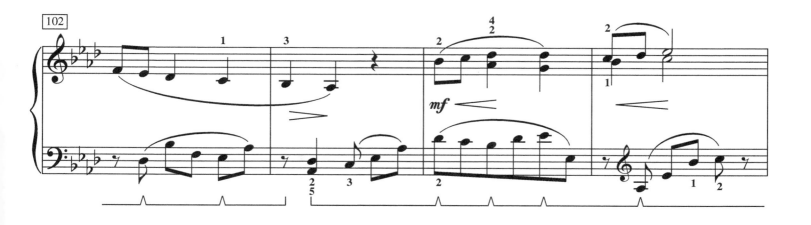

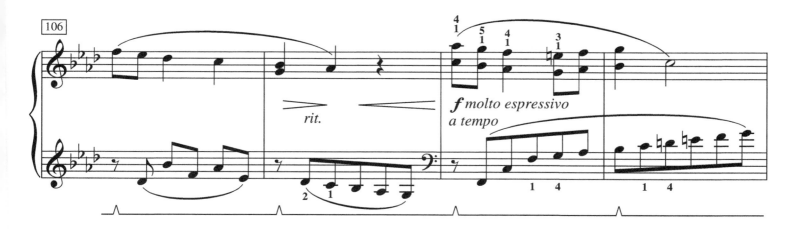

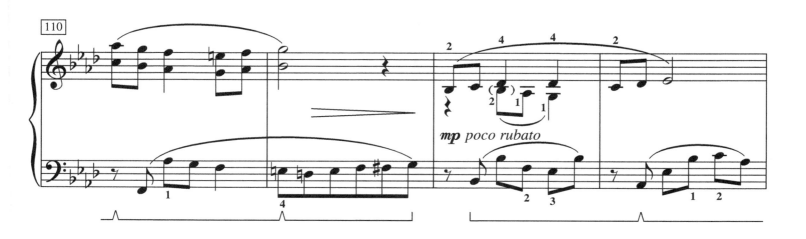

Lullaby, Sweet Jesus
(Lulaj e Jezuniu)
Adagietto cantabile

13

Christis Born (Gdy Si Chrystus Rodzi)
Andante maestoso

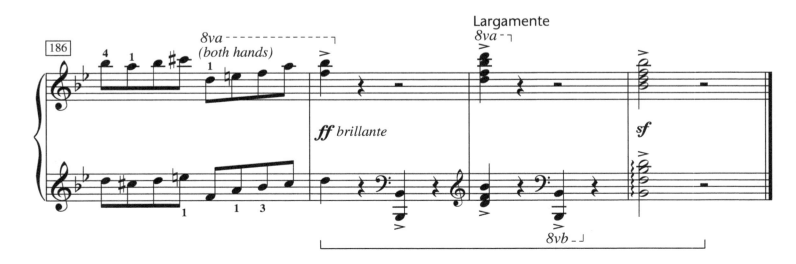